BEING ME IS ENOUGH

When I choose me,
I choose Thee

LWI Publishing Services

Printed in the United States of America
First Printing: May 2019
Second Printing: July 2023

DEDICATION

To my brothers, the ones I know and the ones I don't.

This is a reminder to stay motivated and encouraged on your journey through life. Life can present us men with challenges, setbacks, and moments of doubt, but I want you to know that you have incredible strength within you.
As men of God, we are called to be leaders, not only in our own lives but also in our families, communities, and the world around us. Embrace this responsibility with humility, knowing that true leadership is rooted in service, compassion, and a genuine love for others. Stay rooted in the truth of God's promises.
Even in the midst of difficulties, doubts, and trials, remember that He is faithful and His plans for you are good. Trust in His timing and sovereignty, knowing that He will never leave you nor forsake you.
Take time for personal reflection and spiritual renewal. Cultivate a deep and intimate relationship with God, nourishing your soul through prayer, worship, and study. Remember that God has equipped you with unique gifts and talents for His divine purpose. Seek His guidance in discovering and utilizing these gifts to impact the lives of others and bring glory to His name.
Let your actions speak louder than your words, reflecting the character of Christ in all that you do.

ACKNOWLEDGMENTS

To my wife Lisa, my earthly rock! You inspire me to be a better man in every way. Thank you for showing me what intentional and unconditional love looks like. I truly adore you my love.

To my children; Antionette, my mini-me; Imani, my food and snacks adversary; and Amare', my YouTube loving, gymnastics phenom. You guys make me work even harder to leave a legacy for you to carry forward and build upon for your children. I love you all dearly.

To my mom, Mary, who raised me to understand that there are many levels to being a man of character, I miss you more than words can ever say.

To my pops, Frank, for planting a seed in me that grew into my love for football and my passion for my beloved Cleveland Browns!!

To my siblings, Henry, Jerry and Sabrina, who always pushed me to be the very best I could be at whatever I aspired to do. Thanks for always looking up to me, even though I'm the baby of the bunch. I love you.

And finally, to my dawgs, Rodney, KC and Orvin; my military friends who became my life-long brothers. Our lives are forever connected and I'm so proud of the men you have become. Thanks for always being there and supporting me through all the madness that is the life and times of T-Bone!!!
ONE!!!!!

My Word is Bond

Isaiah 55:11
so is my word that goes out from my mouth: It will not return to me empty, but will accomplish what I desire and achieve the purpose for which I sent it.

My word is bond. As men, integrity is the root of everything we do; both in business and in our personal lives. All we really have is our word just as God stated His Word will never come back void, neither should ours.

Staying true to our word can propel us to heights we never thought possible. Conversely, not staying true to our word can destroy everything we have worked so hard to build. "My word is bond" is more than just a hip-hop cultural saying. It is the foundation that I will build upon.

God has given me the ability to use my words, as he used his ... to build, to love, to encourage, to uplift, to create.

Let's Work

Colossians 3:23
Whatever you do, work at it with all your heart, as working for the Lord, not for human masters,

I will remember, whether as an employee or an employer, my work is for God. As long as I remember who I honor in my hard work, I should never fall short in my efforts.

The plans of the diligent lead to profit as surely as haste leads to poverty. Proverbs 21:5

I was Created to be a Led Leader

Philippians 2:7
rather, he made himself nothing by taking the very nature of a servant, being made in human likeness.

Jesus spent 33 years as a humble follower and leader. He followed his Father in all things and lead His disciples according to His Father's Word.

I must be willing to be humble enough to know God is the ultimate leader that will give me instructions and the ability to lead my family to victory.
In order to lead I must be willing to be led.
I must be willing to serve.

Problem Solved!

I realize in order to make a change, my voice can't just be an echo to the complaint but an individual that foresees the complaint coming and already has a solution.

That solution is God. As the challenges arise, there is a necessary space that I must dwell, a faithful space, a space where He and I meet. God is the ultimate problem solver. All it takes is for me to ask the question and be still enough to hear and receive the answer.

Being Me Is Enough

Luke 10:27
Love the Lord your God with all your heart and with all your soul and with all your strength and with all your mind; and, love your neighbor as yourself

**Never negotiate your relationship with God,
He will never negotiate His relationship with you.**

Success

Genesis 39:2
The Lord was with Joseph so that he prospered, and he lived in the house of his Egyptian master.

My success is not contingent on someone else's downfall.
My success is not contingent on how many likes I get.
My success is not contingent on how many titles I have behind my name.
My success is not contingent on what by bank account looks like, the house in live in or the car I drive.
My success is contingent on having God with me. Like Joseph if I have God with me, I will be successful in all things.

Jesus Wept too

John 11:33-35
When Jesus saw her weeping, and the Jews who had come along with her also weeping, he was deeply moved in spirit and troubled. "Where have you laid him?" he asked. "Come and see, Lord," they replied. Jesus wept.

Showing my emotions does not make me weak. There is strength in my ability to love beyond myself. There is power in my ability to shed tears for my brothers and sisters. There is courage in my ability to forgive my enemies; and there is valor in my ability to forgive myself. Showing my emotions does not make me weak, showing my emotions makes me a man.

My Authority

John 14:12
Very truly I tell you, whoever believes in me will do the works I have been doing, and they will do even greater things than these, because I Am going to the Father.

I Am powerful.

My power comes from more than just my physical, my power comes from within, the part of me that pushes passed pain, sees passed fear, drinks in knowledge as if it were my last breath and perceives obstacles as opportunities to watch my God work in me, through me and around me.

A Change is Coming

God's permanent change in me is way better than any temporary change I attempt to implement on my own. Without Him I am nothing but with him I Am whatever He declares me to be.

Being Me Is Enough

John 3:16 & 17
For God so loved the world that he gave his one and only Son, that
whoever believes in him shall not perish but have eternal life
.

God doesn't love you to death,
He loves you to life.

I Am Indeed the Father

Psalm 103:13
As a father has compassion on his children, so the Lord has compassion on those who fear him.

If I'm bold enough to make a child, then I'll be intentional in being a father; strong enough to raise a king and sensitive enough to raise a queen.

Let us never forget what a gift it is to be a parent. What a privilege and blessing it is to share the same title as God - Father.

Start children off on the way they should go, and even when they are old they will not turn from it. Proverbs 22:6

The Journey

Don't forget to enjoy the journey. We all have a destination, and the destination will come, but until then enjoy the benefits of the journey. There is far too much to learn and experience along the way. Remember to enjoy and embrace every single moment.

Not My Fight but His

Deuteronomy 20:4
For the Lord your God is he who goes with you to fight for you against your enemies, to give you the victory.

Every battle is not yours to fight. Just because it is being presented to you doesn't mean you have to entertain it. Some battles will strengthen you; some will distract you and some have nothing to do with you and will just waste time and energy you will never get back.

Choose your battles wisely. Better yet before choosing any battle, ask God first.

The Lord will fight for you; you need only to be still.
Exodus 14:14

no weapon forged against you will prevail, and you will refute every tongue that accuses you. This is the heritage of the servants of the Lord, and this is their vindication from me," declares the Lord. Isaiah 54:17

A Better Me

Every day I strive to be better than who I was yesterday. Every day is a new day with a new opportunity to see something different even in myself. What was my perception of a personal weakness yesterday has the potential to be a strength for me today.

Being Me Is Enough

Matthew 11:28
Come to me, all you who are weary and burdened, and I will give you rest.

When you leave your bags with the father, DO NOT go back to get them, He knows better than you on how to handle them.

Fear Not

Psalm 56:3-4
When I am afraid, I put my trust in you. In God, whose word I praise — in God I trust and am not afraid. What can mere mortals do to me?

Feeling fear is a natural thing, it doesn't make me less of a man or less of a human.

God knew we would feel FEAR, which is why He said, in Isaiah 41:10 "Fear not, for I am with you; be not dismayed, for I am your God; I will strengthen you, I will help you, I will uphold you with my righteous right hand."

In those times when I am afraid, I will remember that God has not left me and never will. He is my strength and my shield.

For God has not given us a spirit of fear, but of power and of love and of a sound mind. 2 Timothy 1:7

So we say with confidence, "The Lord is my helper; I will not be afraid. What can mere mortals do to me?"
Hebrews 13:6

His Plan, My Purpose

Jeremiah 29:11
"For I know the plans I have for you," declares the LORD, "plans to prosper you and not to harm you, plans to give you hope and a future."

When I can't find my way or when I am struggling with my purpose, I will trust in God to show me the way. In Psalm 32:8, His Word says, "I will instruct you and teach you in the way you should go; I will counsel you with my loving eye on you."

As I embark on the journey that God has for me, I will trust Him even if it doesn't make sense.

Trust in the Lord with all your heart and lean not on your own understanding; in all your ways submit to him, and he will make your paths straight. Proverbs 3:5-6

The Builder

Romans 12:10
Be kindly affectionate to one another with brotherly love, in honor giving preference to one another

I Am a Builder.

I build:
relationships
business deals
families
leaders
bridges
trust
faith
hopes
dreams

bearing with one another, and forgiving one another, if anyone has a complaint against another; even as Christ forgave you, so you also must do. Colossians 3:13

The Decision Maker

Proverbs 18:15
The heart of the discerning acquires knowledge, for the ears of the wise seek it out.

I Am a DECISION MAKER.

The decisions I make don't just affect me. When deciding, I not only decide my fate but OFTENTIMES, the fate of those closest to me. The best part about my DECISION MAKING is that it's not mine alone, I have a helper that walks with me and talks with me. I Am a decision-maker who is connected to the one that has the answers to all DECISIONS. All I have to do is listen and be obedient.

Get wisdom, get understanding; do not forget my words or turn away from them. Proverbs 4:5

Show me your ways, LORD, teach me your paths. Psalms 25:4

Being Me Is Enough

1 Corinthians 16:13
Be on your guard; stand firm in the faith; be courageous; be strong.

If you have to stand on something, stand on God's Word, it will NEVER fail you, it will NEVER come back void.

Time to Work

Psalm 128:2
You will eat the fruit of your labor; blessings and prosperity will be yours.

I Am a Hard Worker.

Though I may work hard, I ensure that I work smart. Unnecessary steps don't serve me any justice unless the goal is to merely look busy.

All hard work brings a profit, but mere talk leads only to poverty.
Proverbs 14:23

It's All about the Hustle

Proverbs 13:4
A sluggard's appetite is never filled, but the desires of the diligent are fully satisfied.

I Am a Hustler.

As long as I have breath in lungs, I will continue to hustle.

Diligent hands will rule, but laziness ends in forced labor. Proverbs 12:24

We Are Kings

Revelation 1:6
and has made us to be a kingdom and priests to serve his God and
Father—to him be glory and power for ever and ever! Amen.

I Am a king among kings.

We are Kings because the ultimate King appointed us to be so. For as He is, so are we.

We are Kings because it is in our DNA.

We are Kings because we are a part of the royal family.

We are Kings because we are heirs to the throne.

We are Kings because we have The King on the inside of us.

You have made them to be a kingdom and priests to serve our
God, and they will reign on the earth. Revelation 5:10

I Will Provide for My Family

1 Timothy 5:8
Anyone who does not provide for their relatives, and especially for their own household, has denied the faith and is worse than an unbeliever.

I Am a Provider.

Providing goes beyond finances. I have the ability to provide support, love, encouragement, motivation, and security. There is no limit to what I can provide at any given moment.

As God provides for us as individuals, we are to share the blessings. Our provision is our neighbor's provision.

And my God will meet all your needs according to the riches of his glory in Christ Jesus. Philippians 4:19

Being Me Is Enough

Matthew 7:7
Ask and it will be given to you; seek and you will find; knock and the door will be opened to you.

Ask Him.

He'll answer.

I Am because He Is

I Am a source of strength for the people in my life. When in need I Am that guy, when having DOUBTS, I Am that guy, when feeling scared I Am that guy, when feeling vulnerable I Am that guy.

I Am Growing

2 Peter 3:18
But grow in the grace and knowledge of our Lord and Savior Jesus Christ. To him be glory both now and forever! Amen.

I was not created to be mediocre.

Mediocrity is not an option; I will consistently and continuously remain in a state of growing and evolving.

The righteous will flourish like a palm tree, they will grow like a cedar of Lebanon; planted in the house of the Lord, they will flourish in the courts of our God. They will still bear fruit in old age, they will stay fresh and green, Psalms 92:12-14

I Will Glorify Him

1 Corinthians 10:31
So, whether you eat or drink, or whatever you do, do all to the glory of God.

In all things someone is getting glory.

Will I attempt to claim the glory, or will I glorify God?

I Am committed to making choices that glorify God.

As I move throughout my day, I want to glorify Him. My words, my choices, my actions should glorify Him.

God and God alone, deserves all the glory, all the honor and all the praise.

"Worthy are you, our Lord and God, to receive glory and honor and power, for you created all things, and by your will they existed and were created." Revelation 4:11

Not to us, O Lord, not to us, but to your name give glory, for the sake of your steadfast love and your faithfulness! Psalm 115:1

Greater is He that is in Me

1 John 4:4
You, dear children, are from God and have overcome them,
because the one who is in you is greater than the one who is in the
world.

I Am filled with greatness.

I Am literally filled with greatness!

Because of the greatness that is within me, I will stand with conviction, walk with intention and speak with assurance.

So God created mankind in his own image, in the image of God he created them; male and female he created them. God blessed them and said to them, "Be fruitful and increase in number; fill the earth and subdue it. Rule over the fish in the sea and the birds in the sky and over every living creature that moves on the ground."
Genesis 1:27-28

Being Me Is Enough

Proverbs 15:29
The Lord is far from the wicked, but he hears the prayer of the righteous.

YES!

He hears you.

YES!

He's listening.

YES!

He cares.

I Am a Winner

1 Corinthians 15:57
But thanks be to God! He gives us the victory through our Lord Jesus Christ.

I Am a winner because He said so.

I Am here to win. Win at life, win at love. win at winning souls for the kingdom.

for everyone born of God overcomes the world. This is the victory that has overcome the world, even our faith. 1 John 5:4

Can I just be honest?

2 Corinthians 8:21
For we are taking pains to do what is right, not only in the eyes of the Lord but also in the eyes of man.

I Am honest; though I may lie to others some I may consider justifiable and some I may not, it truly doesn't do me any service if I lie to myself.

Lying lips are an abomination to the Lord, but those who act faithfully are his delight. Proverbs 12:22

Whoever walks in integrity walks securely, but he who makes his ways crooked will be found out. Proverbs 10:9

Control

Proverbs 14:29
Whoever is patient has great understanding, but one who is quick-tempered displays folly.

I Am in control of my emotions. I will allow myself to feel whatever emotion comes my way, the key is to not allow the emotion so much control that I lose control. Even Jesus got angry but remember the Word says in Ecclesiastes 7:9, "Do not be quickly provoked in your spirit, for anger resides in the lap of fools."

A gentle answer turns away wrath, but a harsh word stirs up anger. Proverbs 15:1

A wrathful man stirs up strife: but he that is slow to anger appeases strife. Proverbs 15:18

Better a patient person than a warrior, one with self-control than one who takes a city. Proverbs 16:32

Love

Romans 5:8
But God demonstrates his own love for us in this: While we were still sinners, Christ died for us.

I Am loved.
I Am loved unconditionally by God.

God is Love.
God resides in Me.
Love is in Me.

We love because he first loved us. 1 John 4:19

The Lord appeared to us in the past, saying, "I have loved you with an everlasting love; I have drawn you with unfailing kindness. Jeremiah 31:3

Being Me Is Enough

Ephesians 6:11 NIV
Put on the full armor of God, so that you can take your stand against the devil's schemes.

There is no greater fashion statement than the Armor of God.

I Know where my Loyalty lies

Proverbs 18:24
One who has unreliable friends soon comes to ruin, but there is a friend who sticks closer than a brother.

I Am loyal to the One.
Where He is, is where I want to be.
Where He goes, is where I want to go.
What's pleasing to Him is what is pleasing to me.

No one can serve two masters, for either he will hate the one and love the other, or he will be devoted to the one and despise the other. You cannot serve God and money. Matthew 6:24

I Will Not Compare

I Am more than enough. My life will not be lived in comparison to anyone else. I was created to be the best version of me that I can be. I can learn from another's journey, but the goal isn't to be that person but to be me with a bit of inspiration from those I encounter that have gone where I intend to go.

I Am More Than

Romans 8:37
No, in all these things we are more than conquerors through him who loved us.

I Am more than what the world sees on the news; regardless of what their perception is, I must remember that when Christ sees me, it is through the lens of the cross that He sees me.

Don't you know that you yourselves are God's temple and that God's Spirit dwells in your midst? 1 Corinthians 3:16

Never a failure

Psalm 37:23-24
The Lord makes firm the steps of the one who delights in him;
though he may stumble, he will not fall, for the Lord upholds him
with his hand.

I Am not a failure. When I have ever "failed", the end result of it was never failure but evidence that I tried and more importantly of God's grace in sustaining me throughout my journey.

The Lord upholds all who fall and lifts up all who are bowed down.
Psalm 145:14

"Say to them, 'This is what the Lord says: "'When people fall down, do they not get up? When someone turns away, do they not return?" Jeremiah 8:4

for though the righteous fall seven times, they rise again, but the wicked stumble when calamity strikes. Proverbs 24:16

Being Me Is Enough

o me, "My grace is sufficient for you, for my power is made perfect in weakness." Therefore I will boast all the more gladly about my weaknesses, so that Christ's power may rest on me.

You are enough and God is more than enough.

Things

Colossians 3:2
Set your minds on things above, not on earthly things.

I will not be controlled by the material items I want or have. I am reminded that I Am to be focused on things that are everlasting.

Do not store up for yourselves treasures on earth, where moths and vermin destroy, and where thieves break in and steal. But store up for yourselves treasures in heaven, where moths and vermin do not destroy, and where thieves do not break in and steal. For where your treasure is, there your heart will be also.
Matthew 6:19-21

First things first

Matthew 6:33
But seek first his kingdom and his righteousness, and all these things will be given to you as well.

In all things, big and small, I will seek God first.

As an employee, you would never walk into a company and make CEO moves at least not without getting permission/direction from the CEO first.

As a business owner, you still have to consult with someone or something to ensure you are within the rules and regulations of your space to ensure you maximize your efforts and results.

In all things we should consult with the ultimate CEO of our lives.

Life is so much easier with instruction and direction.

But seek His kingdom, and these things will be given to you as well.
Luke 12:31

My Character

Romans 8:14
For those who are led by the Spirit of God are the children of God.

I will not be defined by the title given to me by the world; my focus is to ensure my character is in line with Christ's character.

Not only so, but we also glory in our sufferings, because we know that suffering produces perseverance; perseverance, character; and character, hope. Romans 5:3-4

Every Day I Am a Little Closer

Proverbs 16:9
In their hearts humans plan their course, but the Lord establishes their steps.

With Gods' guidance, every day I Am that much closer to reaching my goals. Every step I take should be according to His instruction. Regardless of how many steps it takes, and how many distractions come my way, I will keep moving forward till I hit the mark. No matter how often I make plans, His plans are always greater than mine.

Many are the plans in a person's heart, but it is the Lord's purpose that prevails. Proverbs 19:21

Being Me Is Enough

Ecclesiastes 1:9 NIV
The eye never has enough of seeing, nor the ear its fill of hearing. 9 What has been will be again, what has been done will be done again; there is nothing new under the sun.

Remember there is nothing new under the sun so when you go before Him, He won't be surprised, He's seen it all and by the way, Jesus died for that thing too.

Reaping

Psalm 128:2
You will eat the fruit of your labor; blessings and prosperity will be yours.

Hard work, when coupled with a heart devoted to righteousness, leads to blessings and a life filled with contentment. Those who invest their efforts in honest work can expect to enjoy the fruits of their labor and experience the favor and goodness of the Lord.

The blessing of the Lord brings wealth, without painful toil for it.
Proverbs 10:22

I Will Be Open

Lamentations 3:22-23
Because of the Lord's great love we are not consumed, for his compassions never fail. They are new every morning; great is your faithfulness.

I will be open to receive love, God's love; the kind of love that will uplift me, the kind that will leave me with the desire to be better and do better, the kind that will love me to the point that I begin to love myself.

I have told you this so that my joy may be in you and that your joy may be complete. John 15:11

Brotherhood

I Am part of a brotherhood. Brotherhood is a powerful and meaningful concept that emphasizes the importance of unity, support, and mutual care, fostering a sense of kinship and belonging among individuals who share a common bond.

Words

I must always remember the power of my words. God created the world in 6 days using His words. I must remember, just as easily as I can build things and people with my words, I can also tear down and destroy.

Being Me Is Enough

Psalm 34:1 ESV
I will bless the LORD at all times; his praise shall continually be in my mouth.

Be sure to let your praise be authentically yours. God wants your praise, not someone else's.

Out of My Mind

Proverbs 29:25
Fear of man will prove to be a snare, but whoever trusts in the Lord is kept safe.

I cannot be concerned with the opinions of people if God is my focus. It is dangerous to be so concerned with what others think of me that it moves me further from the man God created me to be.

It is better to take refuge in the LORD than to trust in humans. Psalm 118:8

If we are "out of our mind," as some say, it is for God; if we are in our right mind, it is for you. 2 Corinthians 5:13

Valued

I Am valued. My value is not based on the economy, nor the Dow Jones. My value doesn't fluctuate. My value is found in God's love for me which never wavers.

I Am Chosen

Ephesians 1:4-5
just as He chose us in Him before the foundation of the world, that we would be holy and blameless before Him. In love He predestined us to adoption as sons through Jesus Christ to Himself, according to the kind intention of His will,

I Am Chosen

But you are a chosen people, a royal priesthood, a holy nation, God's special possession, that you may declare the praises of him who called you out of darkness into his wonderful light. 1 Peter 2:9

You did not choose me, but I chose you and appointed you so that you might go and bear fruit—fruit that will last—and so that whatever you ask in my name the Father will give you. John 15:16

Move

Matthew 17:20
He replied, "Because you have so little faith. Truly I tell you, if you have faith as small as a mustard seed, you can say to this mountain, 'Move from here to there,' and it will move. Nothing will be impossible for you."

I can move mountains.

He replied, "If you have faith as small as a mustard seed, you can say to this mulberry tree, 'Be uprooted and planted in the sea,' and it will obey you. Luke 17:6

Now to him who is able to do immeasurably more than all we ask or imagine, according to his power that is at work within us, Ephesians 3:20

Being Me Is Enough

1 John 4:9 & 10 NIV
This is how God showed his love among us: He sent his one and only Son into the world that we might live through him. 10 This is love: not that we loved God, but that he loved us and sent his Son as an atoning sacrifice for our sins.

Pause for a moment and listen, God is telling you how much He loves you right now.

God equips the called

Exodus 4:10-11
Moses said to the LORD, "Pardon your servant, Lord. I have never been eloquent, neither in the past nor since you have spoken to your servant. I am slow of speech and tongue."
The LORD said to him, "Who gave human beings their mouths? Who makes them deaf or mute? Who gives them sight or makes them blind? Is it not I, the LORD?

I no longer need validation to know who I Am.
God has already validated me.

for it is God who works in you to will and to act in order to fulfill his good purpose. Philippians 2:13

Each of you should use whatever gift you have received to serve others, as faithful stewards of God's grace in its various forms. 1 Peter 4:10

Honor, the lost art

Romans 12:10
Be devoted to one another in love. Honor one another above yourselves.

It is my honor to honor in the way God intended.

that all may honor the Son just as they honor the Father. Whoever does not honor the Son does not honor the Father, who sent him. John 5:23

Give to everyone what you owe them: If you owe taxes, pay taxes; if revenue, then revenue; if respect, then respect; if honor, then honor. Romans 13:7

"Honor your father and mother"—which is the first commandment with a promise—Ephesians 6:2

Resist

Matthew 5:38-39
"You have heard that it was said, 'Eye for eye, and tooth for tooth.'
But I tell you, do not resist an evil person. If anyone slaps you on
the right cheek, turn to them the other cheek also.

I know when to stand and when to walk away...walking away doesn't scream defeat more often than not it screams Victory!

Make sure that nobody pays back wrong for wrong, but always strive to do what is good for each other and for everyone else. 1 Thessalonians 5:15

bless those who curse you, pray for those who mistreat you. Luke 6:28

If your enemy is hungry, give him food to eat;
if he is thirsty, give him water to drink. Proverbs 25:21

I Hear You and I Am Listening

Matthew 11:15
Whoever has ears, let them hear.

I will listen with an ear to understand and not just respond. The same way I declare I Am willing to hear what God is saying to me is the same way I must be willing to hear from those He has placed in my life for a moment, a season or a lifetime.

Because he turned his ear to me, I will call on him as long as I live.
Psalm 116:2

Listen to my instruction and be wise; do not disregard it. Proverbs 8:33

Listen and hear my voice; pay attention and hear what I say.
Isaiah 28:23

Being Me Is Enough

Genesis 1:27
So God created mankind in his own image, in the image of God he created them; male and female he created them.

You were made in His image. He gave you the breath of life.
You were created with intention and for a purpose.

Iron Sharpens Iron

Proverbs 27:17
As iron sharpens iron, so one person sharpens another.

I must be willing to be held accountable and I will call on people to hold me accountable when they see me drifting.

Brothers and sisters, if someone is caught in a sin, you who live by the Spirit should restore that person gently. But watch yourselves, or you also may be tempted. Carry each other's burdens, and in this way you will fulfill the law of Christ. Galatians 6:1-2

The way of fools seems right to them,
but the wise listen to advice. Proverbs 12:15

Therefore confess your sins to each other and pray for each other so that you may be healed. The prayer of a righteous person is powerful and effective. James 5:16

The truth & The Truth

John 8:32
Then you will know the truth, and the truth will set you free.

I have The Truth within me so I must walk in it daily. I will share The Truth, giving everyone an opportunity to know The Truth as I do. But it is not for me to force The Truth onto anyone. All we have to do is to plant the seed, and God will handle the rest.

But when he, the Spirit of truth, comes, he will guide you into all the truth. He will not speak on his own; he will speak only what he hears, and he will tell you what is yet to come. John 16:13

Guide me in your truth and teach me, for you are God my Savior, and my hope is in you all day long. Psalms 25:5

The LORD detests lying lips, but he delights in people who are trustworthy. Proverbs 12:22

With God-like Intensity

John 13:34
A new command I give you: Love one another. As I have loved you, so you must love one another.

I will love INTENTIONALLY in the same way that God loves me. And when I struggle in this space, I will remember that *I can do ALL things*, even love intentionally, *through Christ who strengthens me.*

Love is patient, love is kind. It does not envy, it does not boast, it is not proud. It does not dishonor others, it is not self-seeking, it is not easily angered, it keeps no record of wrongs. Love does not delight in evil but rejoices with the truth. It always protects, always trusts, always hopes, always perseveres. Love never fails. But where there are prophecies, they will cease; where there are tongues, they will be stilled; where there is knowledge, it will pass away. 1 Corinthians 13:4-8

8 Above all, love each other deeply, because love covers over a multitude of sins. 1Peter 4:8

Distractions

Proverbs 4:25-27
Let your eyes look straight ahead; fix your gaze directly before you. Give careful thought to the paths for your feet and be steadfast in all your ways. 27 Do not turn to the right or the left; keep your foot from evil.

I will not allow myself to get distracted and lose focus. Distractions cause unnecessary and avoidable delays and time is something one can never get back.

Be very careful, then, how you live—not as unwise but as wise, making the most of every opportunity, because the days are evil. Ephesians 5:15-16

Be alert and of sober mind. Your enemy the devil prowls around like a roaring lion looking for someone to devour. 1 Peter 5:8

Teach me your way, LORD, that I may rely on your faithfulness; give me an undivided heart, that I may fear your name. Psalm 86:11

Being Me Is Enough

Jeremiah 29:11
For I know the plans I have for you," declares the LORD, "plans to prosper you and not to harm you, plans to give you hope and a future.

Many of us are striving just to BE.
Do you want to BE?
Then be who God created you to BE.

Mr. Pride

Proverbs 11:2
When pride comes, then comes disgrace, but with humility comes wisdom.

I will not allow pride to block me from my blessings, my lessons, my message, or my purpose.

Pride goes before destruction, a haughty spirit before a fall. Proverbs 16:18

In his pride the wicked man does not seek him; in all his thoughts there is no room for God. Psalms 10:4

For by the grace given me I say to every one of you: Do not think of yourself more highly than you ought, but rather think of yourself with sober judgment, in accordance with the faith God has distributed to each of you. Romans 12:3

Live in harmony with one another. Do not be proud, but be willing to associate with people of low position. Do not be conceited. Romans 12:16

Just Ask

Matthew 7:7
Ask, and it will be given to you; seek, and you will find; knock, and it will be opened to you.

I will not be afraid to ask for help and more importantly I will not be afraid to accept help when offered.

My help comes from the Lord, who made heaven and earth. Psalm 121:2

Until now you have not asked for anything in my name. Ask and you will receive, and your joy will be complete. John 16:24

I Am Not Worried

Psalm 55:22
Cast your cares on the Lord and he will sustain you; he will never let the righteous be shaken.

Worrying SERVES me no purpose. My God is waiting patiently for me to cast my cares onto Him. He is the ultimate care taker. He is the answer to all my CONCERNS. I will no longer carry a load that my Father is willing to take for me and from me.

When I am afraid, I put my trust in you. Psalm 56:3

When anxiety was great within me, your consolation brought joy to my soul. Psalm 94:19

Look at the birds of the air; they do not sow or reap or store away in barns, and yet your heavenly Father feeds them. Are you not much more valuable than they? Matthew 6:26

I Am Not Alone

Psalm 145:18-19
The Lord is near to all who call on him, to all who call on him in truth. He fulfills the desires of those who fear him; he hears their cry and saves them.

The enemy wants me to believe that I am alone, but God said He would never leave me nor forsake me. His Word never comes back void. I will forever stand on His promises.

Be strong and courageous. Do not be afraid or terrified because of them, for the Lord your God goes with you; he will never leave you nor forsake you. Deuteronomy 31:6

So do not fear, for I am with you; do not be dismayed, for I am your God. I will strengthen you and help you; I will uphold you with my righteous right hand. Isaiah 41:10

When you pass through the waters, I will be with you; and when you pass through the rivers, they will not sweep over you. When you walk through the fire, you will not be burned; the flames will not set you ablaze. Isaiah 43:2

Being Me Is Enough

2 Corinthians 5:17
Therefore if any man be in Christ, he is a new creature: old things are passed away; behold, all things are become new.

You may or may not know what they say, but what does God say?

Let us remain focused on that.

Slow to Anger

Psalm 37:8
Refrain from anger and turn from wrath; do not fret—it leads only to evil.

I will not be quick to anger. My anger does not guarantee an understanding, nor does it guarantee me being heard. I will remember that a quick reaction may make a permanent decision off of a temporary feeling.

An angry person stirs up conflict, and a hot-tempered person commits many sins. Proverbs 29:22

Whoever is patient has great understanding, but one who is quick-tempered displays folly. Proverbs 14:29

But you, Lord, are a compassionate and gracious God, slow to anger, abounding in love and faithfulness. Psalm 86:15

My Talents

James 1:17
Every good and perfect gift is from above, coming down from the Father of the heavenly lights, who does not change like shifting shadows.

I will not undervalue myself. If I don't see the value in my talents and gifts, then how could I possibly use them for what God intended? It is all for His glory and God gets no glory in me downplaying or hiding my gifts; they were given to me by God.

For we are God's handiwork, created in Christ Jesus to do good works, which God prepared in advance for us to do. Ephesians 2:10

Each of you should use whatever gift you have received to serve others, as faithful stewards of God's grace in its various forms. If anyone speaks, they should do so as one who speaks the very words of God. If anyone serves, they should do so with the strength God provides, so that in all things God may be praised through Jesus Christ. To him be the glory and the power for ever and ever. Amen. 1 Peter 4:10-11

My People

Proverbs 13:20
Walk with the wise and become wise, for a companion of fools suffers harm.

I will surround myself with people who help me to be a better me; I Am still a work in progress.

Do not be misled: "Bad company corrupts good character." 1 Corinthians 15:33

Wounds from a friend can be trusted, but an enemy multiplies kisses. Proverbs 27:6

One who has unreliable friends soon comes to ruin, but there is a friend who sticks closer than a brother. Proverbs 18:24

Obedience

Luke 11:28
He replied, "Blessed rather are those who hear the word of God and obey it."

I will take the position that God intended for me to have. I will go in the way that God would have me to go. And I will do what it is that God would have me to do in the way that He would have me to do it.

You are my friends if you do what I command. John 15:14

As obedient children, do not conform to the evil desires you had when you lived in ignorance. 1 Peter 1:14

Being Me Is Enough

1 Timothy 3:4-5
He must manage his own family well and see that his children obey him, and he must do so in a manner worthy of full respect. (If anyone does not know how to manage his own family, how can he take care of God's church?)

As the head of your household, if your word is final why is God's say not final? He is the head of all of His children's households.

I Will Not Conform

Romans 12:2
Do not conform to the pattern of this world, but be transformed by the renewing of your mind. Then you will be able to test and approve what God's will is—his good, pleasing and perfect will.

I'm not defined by the world's view of me. I will not conform to the world just so I can fit in. Once I accepted Jesus as my personal Lord and Savior, I have been set apart; not above or below but apart.

Do not love the world or anything in the world. If anyone loves the world, love for the Father is not in them. 1 John 2:15

Set your minds on things above, not on earthly things. Colossians 3:2

I Delight in My Vulnerability

2 Corinthians 12:9-10
But he said to me, "My grace is sufficient for you, for my power is made perfect in weakness." Therefore I will boast all the more gladly about my weaknesses, so that Christ's power may rest on me. That is why, for Christ's sake, I delight in weaknesses, in insults, in hardships, in persecutions, in difficulties. For when I am weak, then I am strong.

It is ok for me to be vulnerable with those that are worthy of my vulnerability. Only through vulnerability can someone see my heart.

Then Peter came to Jesus and asked, "Lord, how many times shall I forgive my brother when he sins against me? Up to seven times?" Jesus answered, "I tell you, not seven times, but seventy-seven times. Matthew 18:21-22

I Believe

John 11:40
Then Jesus said, "Did I not tell you that if you believe, you will see the glory of God?"

No matter what it looks like, no matter what the world says, I have faith in the God that I serve and that is all that I need.

Now faith is confidence in what we hope for and assurance about what we do not see. Hebrews 11:1

And without faith it is impossible to please God, because anyone who comes to him must believe that he exists and that he rewards those who earnestly seek him. Hebrews 11:6

For no word from God will ever fail. Luke 1:37

My Race to Run

Philippians 3:12
Not that I have already obtained all this, or have already arrived at my goal, but I press on to take hold of that for which Christ Jesus took hold of me.

My race is my race to run and no one else's. I Am my own competition.

I press on toward the goal to win the prize for which God has called me heavenward in Christ Jesus. Philippians 3:14

However, I consider my life worth nothing to me; my only aim is to finish the race and complete the task the Lord Jesus has given me–the task of testifying to the good news of God's grace. Acts 20:24

Being Me Is Enough

Proverbs 16:18
Pride goes before destruction, a haughty spirit before a fall.

Pride
Playing
right
into
the devil's
ego
Pride cometh before the fall.

The Clock is Ticking

Proverbs 27:1
Do not boast about tomorrow, for you do not know what a day may bring.

My time is valuable, I will not waste it. One of the most important assets I have is time. Once it is used, I can never get it back. People will only place as much value on my time as I demand. I will not allow others to take advantage of my time including myself.

As long as it is day, we must do the works of him who sent me. Night is coming, when no one can work. John 9:4

And do this, understanding the present time: The hour has already come for you to wake up from your slumber, because our salvation is nearer now than when we first believed. Romans 13:11

"But about that day or hour no one knows, not even the angels in heaven, nor the Son, but only the Father.
Be on guard! Be alert! You do not know when that time will come. Mark 13:32-33

The Journey

Psalm 128:2
You will eat the fruit of your labor; blessings and prosperity will be yours.

There are no limitations to the greatness that is within me. I will never let NO stop you from the path God has for me. I will never be afraid to present an idea.

Who would have thought that people would have minicomputers for phones? Steve Jobs, former CEO of Apple.
Who would have thought that people would spend $5 and more for a cup of coffee? Jerry Baldwin, Zev Siegl and Gordon Bowker, Founders of Starbucks.

Think of a world without Apple and Starbucks. Now, think of a world without you. What great ideas would the world be missing out on? Whatever your business idea, if you believe in it, present it.

The blessing of the Lord brings wealth, without painful toil for it.
Proverbs 10:22

My Silence

Proverbs 17:28
Even fools are thought wise if they keep silent, and discerning if they hold their tongues.

There is power is my silence. We constantly ask questions, but rarely are silent long enough to hear the answers. I will intentionally sit in silence and listen for the answers that I seek. I will sit in silence, at His feet, and wait to receive instruction on how I should move, and only then will I move with intention and confidence.

a time to tear and a time to mend, a time to be silent and a time to speak Ecclesiastes 3:7

To answer before listening—that is folly and shame. Proverbs 18:13

Be Bold

Will you play it safe and go for the tie, or will you be bold and go for the win? Greatness doesn't come from playing is safe; greatness comes from being bold and walking in your authority. It comes from being obedient to God's Word and direction and knowing who has your back. Condition yourself to always go forward in that authority. When God says move, move with boldness.

He proclaimed the Kingdom of God and taught about the Lord Jesus Christ - with all boldness and without hinderance! Acts 28:31

The wicked flee though no one pursues, but the righteous are as bold as a lion. Proverbs 28:1

Let us then approach God's throne of grace with confidence, so that we may receive mercy and find grace to help us in our time of need. Hebrews 4:16

Being Me Is Enough

1 John 3:6
No one who lives in him keeps on sinning. No one who continues to sin has either seen Him or known Him.

Do you know of God, or do you know God?

I Count it All Joy

James 1:2-8
Consider it pure joy, my brothers and sisters, whenever you face trials of many kinds, because you know that the testing of your faith produces perseverance. Let perseverance finish its work so that you may be mature and complete, not lacking anything. If any of you lacks wisdom, you should ask God, who gives generously to all without finding fault, and it will be given to you. But when you ask, you must believe and not doubt, because the one who doubts is like a wave of the sea, blown and tossed by the wind. That person should not expect to receive anything from the Lord. Such a person is double-minded and unstable in all they do.

I will not allow hiccups to stop me. Trials and tribulations are a part of the process, without them I wouldn't know all that God could do and be for me, and all that I am in Him. All things serve its purpose for the glory of the Lord.

Blessed is the one who perseveres under trial because, having stood the test, that person will receive the crown of life that the Lord has promised to those who love him. James 1:12

"I have told you these things, so that in me you may have peace. In this world you will have trouble. But take heart! I have overcome the world." John 16:33

Clean hands, Pure heart

Psalm 24:4-5
The one who has clean hands and a pure heart, who does not trust in an idol or swear by a false god. They will receive blessing from the Lord and vindication from God their Savior.

The goal isn't perfection but to have clean hands and a pure heart.

Create in me a pure heart, O God,
and renew a steadfast spirit within me. Psalm 51:10

How can a young person stay on the path of purity?
By living according to your word. Psalm 119:9

The goal of this command is love, which comes from a pure heart and a good conscience and a sincere faith. 1 Timothy 1:5

My Blessings

I have never heard of a blessing deficit. What God has for me is for me. Regardless of how many blessings I witness other people receiving, I will never worry that there won't be enough for me.

I must also remember to bless others as God blesses me. Just as I could never do enough to be blessed, I should not make it a requirement that I bless others based on their merit.

Wise Counsel

Proverbs 19:20-21
Listen to advice and accept discipline, and at the end you will be counted among the wise. Many are the plans in a person's heart, but it is the Lord's purpose that prevails.

Not only will I be open to receiving advice, but I will be mindful of where that advice comes from. I will be sure to surround myself with wise counsel; not based on my feelings, but on God's guidance.

The way of fools seems right to them, but the wise listen to advice.
Proverbs 12:15

Being Me Is Enough

Romans 3:23-24
For all have sinned and fall short of the glory of God, and all are justified freely by his grace through the redemption that came by Christ Jesus

Guess what?

His grace truly is sufficient.

I Am Not My Past

Micah 7:19
You will again have compassion on us; you will tread our sins underfoot and hurl all our iniquities into the depths of the sea.

God says that He will cast our past sins into the sea of forgetfulness. So, why is it so hard for us to do the same? I will not be bound by the things of my past.

Brothers and sisters, I do not consider myself yet to have taken hold of it. But one thing I do: Forgetting what is behind and straining toward what is ahead, 14 I press on toward the goal to win the prize for which God has called me heavenward in Christ Jesus. Philippians 3:13-14

But God Said

2 Samuel 7:28
Sovereign Lord, you are God! Your covenant is trustworthy, and you have promised these good things to your servant.

I will not listen to what the world says, but what God says. God says I'm rich, regardless of what my bank account says. God says I'm healed regardless of what the doctor says. God says I Am His regardless of what the world says.

Then the woman said to Elijah, "Now I know that you are a man of God and that the word of the Lord from your mouth is the truth." 1 Kings 17:24

Who Cares?

Isaiah 49:13
Shout for joy, you heavens; rejoice, you earth; burst into song, you mountains! For the LORD comforts his people and will have compassion on his afflicted ones.

God does!

While it may seem that everything "self-care" is not geared towards men; who cares for the men?
Who cares when we are hurting?
Who cares when we are struggling?
Who cares when we are lacking confidence?
Who cares when we feel broken?

God does!

Praise be to the God and Father of our Lord Jesus Christ, the Father of compassion and the God of all comfort, 4 who comforts us in all our troubles, so that we can comfort those in any trouble with the comfort we ourselves receive from God. 2 Corinthians 1:3-4

I Don't Need a Stepping Stool

Psalms 119:89-91
Your word, Lord, is eternal; it stands firm in the heavens. Your faithfulness continues through all generations; you established the earth, and it endures. Your laws endure to this day, for all things serve you.

During difficult times, it is the Word of God that I will stand on. When the world tries to beat me down, God's Word is the foundation I will use to steady myself and rise above my circumstance.

So do not fear, for I am with you; do not be dismayed, for I am your God. I will strengthen you and help you; I will uphold you with my righteous right hand. Isaiah 41:10

Being Me Is Enough

Psalm 119:105
Your word is a lamp for my feet, a light on my path." Light is something that is necessary to navigate this world of darkness. We need light to guide us safely through the unforeseen dangers that await us.

This road was never promised to be easy, the promise was for peace, provision, protection, grace, forgiveness, love and a constant companion and guide.

Pick Me Lord

When I start to doubt who I Am and what my purpose is, I am reminded that Jesus chose fishermen, a tax collector, activists and even a murderer to do great things. So, God can use me too.

Not My Time, But His

2 Peter 3:8
But do not forget this one thing, dear friends: With the Lord a day is like a thousand years, and a thousand years are like a day.

As I wait on GOD, I will remember that I am being prepared and positioned for my purpose.

Be still before the Lord and wait patiently for him; do not fret when people succeed in their ways, when they carry out their wicked schemes. Psalms 37:7

He is My Light

Isaiah 60:19-20
The sun will no more be your light by day, nor will the brightness of the moon shine on you, for the Lord will be your everlasting light, and your God will be your glory. Your sun will never set again, and your moon will wane no more; the Lord will be your everlasting light, and your days of sorrow will end.

When it gets DARK, I will remember I have an eternal light to guide me and light my way.

When Jesus spoke again to the people, he said, "I am the light of the world. Whoever follows me will never walk in darkness, but will have the light of life." John 8:12

You, Lord, keep my lamp burning; my God turns my darkness into light. Psalm 18:28

Never Lost

Isaiah 58:11
The Lord will guide you always; he will satisfy your needs in a sun-scorched land and will strengthen your frame.
You will be like a well-watered garden, like a spring whose waters never fail.

Because of God and His promise, I will never be lost. My guide has promised to forever guide me.

For the Son of Man came to seek and to save the lost. Luke 19:10

Being Me Is Enough

Isaiah 4:6
It will be a shelter and shade from the heat of the day, and a refuge and hiding place from the storm and rain.

As you struggle to count it all joy, consider it's often at our lowest point when we realize who we can turn to and who is in our corner. It's in the storm we understand the magnitude of God love and protection for us.

Giving Up is Not an Option

Galatians 6:9
Let us not become weary in doing good, for at the proper time we will reap a harvest if we do not give up.

When I feel like giving up, I'm reminded that God loves me and wants me to live life to the fullest. God's plan for my life is to prosper me and not harm me. With God I am never alone, and he gives me the strength to keep going.

Therefore we do not lose heart. Though outwardly we are wasting away, yet inwardly we are being renewed day by day. For our light and momentary troubles are achieving for us an eternal glory that far outweighs them all. So we fix our eyes not on what is seen, but on what is unseen, since what is seen is temporary, but what is unseen is eternal. 2 Corinthians 4:16-18

Unconditional Love

Lamentations 3:22-23
Because of the Lord's great love we are not consumed, for his compassions never fail. They are new every morning; great is your faithfulness.

If no one else loves me unconditionally, God does. Despite my flaws, He loves me. Despite my mistakes, He loves me. Despite my sins, He loves me. He loves me unconditionally. His love for me is not contingent on how I move, my title, my status nor my finances. His love for me is unconditional.

Because your love is better than life, my lips will glorify you. Psalm 63:3

Give thanks to the Lord, for he is good; his love endures forever. 1 Chronicles 16:34

He Goes Before Me

Deuteronomy 31:8
The Lord himself goes before you and will be with you; he will never leave you nor forsake you. Do not be afraid; do not be discouraged."

I will follow God for He knows the challenges that I will face, and the obstacles and pitfalls before me. Just as Jesus went before me to intercept the judgement of sin with his life, God will go before me to protect me from things unseen.

I will go before you and will level the mountains; I will break down gates of bronze and cut through bars of iron. Isaiah 45:2

to him who led his people through the wilderness; His love endures forever. Psalm 136:16

Be Still

Psalm 37:7
Be still before the Lord and wait patiently for him; do not fret when people succeed in their ways, when they carry out their wicked schemes.

As men, we feel the need to fix, the need to move, the need to respond, the need to react, the need to address, the need, the need, the need.

In His Word God said that He would meet every need and at times we are the vessel used to meet said need. However, there are also times when we need to just be still, so that God can be God.

He got up, rebuked the wind and said to the waves, "Quiet! Be still!" Then the wind died down and it was completely calm. Mark 4:39

The fruit of that righteousness will be peace; its effect will be quietness and confidence forever. Isaiah 32:17

Being Me Is Enough

James 1:17 NIV
Every good and perfect gift is from above, coming down from the Father of the heavenly lights, who does not change like shifting shadows.

What are you doing with your talents?

I Am His Creation

Genesis 2:7
Then the Lord God formed a man from the dust of the ground and breathed into his nostrils the breath of life, and the man became a living being.

I was not created by accident but for a purpose. My journey is bigger than me.

In the beginning was the Word, and the Word was with God, and the Word was God. He was with God in the beginning. Through him all things were made; without him nothing was made that has been made. John 1:1-3

I Am Content

Philippians 4:11
I am not saying this because I am in need, for I have learned to be content whatever the circumstances.

Being content and satisfied doesn't mean I will not strive to be better or desire more, it means that I will never forget that The Lord is my portion, He is my earthly and eternal inheritance.

He chose our inheritance for us, the pride of Jacob, whom he loved. Psalm 47:4

Put It Away

Ephesians 4:31
Get rid of all bitterness, rage and anger, brawling and slander,
along with every form of malice.

I put away bitterness, malice, wrath, anger and evil speaking. I will only speak words of love, life and abundance.

Be kind and compassionate to one another, forgiving each other,
just as in Christ God forgave you. Ephesians 4:32

The Lord Is My Life

Deuteronomy 30:20
and that you may love the Lord your God, listen to his voice, and hold fast to him. For the Lord is your life, and he will give you many years in the land he swore to give to your fathers, Abraham, Isaac and Jacob.

He is my life first so that I can have life and live life. I will listen to His voice and hold onto His every word. I will look to Him in all that I do.

Whom have I in heaven but you? And earth has nothing I desire besides you. My flesh and my heart may fail, but God is the strength of my heart and my portion forever. Psalm 73:25-26

Being Me Is Enough

Revelation 22:13
I am the Alpha and the Omega, the First and the Last, the Beginning and the End.

God is the Alpha and the Omega

God is the Beginning and the End

God is, not man.

Healed & Whole

Jeremiah 33:6
Nevertheless, I will bring health and healing to it; I will heal my people and will let them enjoy abundant peace and security.

I Am healed and whole; God promised it to me. He will heal me and make me whole and allow me to enjoy abundant peace and security.

"Go," said Jesus, "your faith has healed you." Immediately he received his sight and followed Jesus along the road. Mark 10:52

My Future

Psalm 16:5
Lord, you alone are my portion and my cup; you make my lot secure.

My future is secure.

being confident of this, that he who began a good work in you will carry it on to completion until the day of Christ Jesus. Philippians 1:6

My Daily Provision

Philippians 4:19
And my God will meet all your needs according to the riches of his glory in Christ Jesus.

God is my source. He is my daily provision. I will not worry for what tomorrow will bring or what needs need to be met. God has promised that He will provide for me daily.

But you, Lord, are a shield around me, my glory, the One who lifts my head high. Psalm 3:3

Favor

Proverbs 3:4
Then you will win favor and a good name in the sight of God and man.

I have favor with God and man.

May the favor of the Lord our God rest on us; establish the work of our hands for us—yes, establish the work of our hands. Psalm 90:17

Being Me Is Enough

Matthew 14:17-21
We have here only five loaves of bread and two fish," they answered. "Bring them here to me," he said. And he directed the people to sit down on the grass. Taking the five loaves and the two fish and looking up to heaven, he gave thanks and broke the loaves. Then he gave them to the disciples, and the disciples gave them to the people. They all ate and were satisfied, and the disciples picked up twelve basketfuls of broken pieces that were left over. The number of those who ate was about five thousand men, besides women and children.

2 Fish & 5 Loaves

If He did it for them, He will do it for you.

Good Soil

Matthew 13:22-23
The seed falling among the thorns refers to someone who hears the word, but the worries of this life and the deceitfulness of wealth choke the word, making it unfruitful. But the seed falling on good soil refers to someone who hears the word and understands it. This is the one who produces a crop, yielding a hundred, sixty or thirty times what was sown."

I Am good SOIL; I receive the Word with understanding and produce a fruitful crop of love, support, encouragement, motivation and security.

I am the vine; you are the branches. If you remain in me and I in you, you will bear much fruit; apart from me you can do nothing.
John 15:5

Peace

Isaiah 32:18
My people will live in peaceful dwelling places, in secure homes, in undisturbed places of rest.

I Am surrounded by peace. I have peace within me and all around me. The spaces and places that have been created for me are full of peace. These are the places I find rest.

I Am filled with joy and peace.

May the God of hope fill you with all joy and peace as you trust in him, so that you may overflow with hope by the power of the Holy Spirit. Romans 15:13

Bread of Life

John 6:54-57
Whoever eats my flesh and drinks my blood has eternal life, and I will raise them up at the last day. For my flesh is real food and my blood is real drink. Whoever eats my flesh and drinks my blood remains in me, and I in them. Just as the living Father sent me and I live because of the Father, so the one who feeds on me will live because of me.

Man cannot live on bread alone; I feast on what is everlasting. I shall feast on the Word of God daily.

I am the living bread that came down from heaven. Whoever eats this bread will live forever. This bread is my flesh, which I will give for the life of the world." John 6:51

Then Jesus declared, "I am the bread of life. Whoever comes to me will never go hungry, and whoever believes in me will never be thirsty. John 6:35

I Am New

2 Corinthians 5:17
Therefore, if anyone is in Christ, the new creation has come: The old has gone, the new is here!

I Am a new creature in Christ Jesus, the old has gone and the new is here!

See, I will create new heavens and a new earth. The former things will not be remembered, nor will they come to mind. Isaiah 65:17

Being Me Is Enough

Luke 22:42
Father, if you are willing, take this cup from me; yet not my will, but yours be done.

In all things, ask for it to be in His Will.

Darkness Can't Win

I Thessalonians 5:5
You are all children of the light and children of the day. We do not belong to the night or to the darkness.

Darkness will not overtake me because I Am a child of the light. I do not belong to the night or the darkness. Where there is light, darkness cannot survive.

The light shines in the darkness, and the darkness has not overcome it. John 1:5

For you were once darkness, but now you are light in the Lord. Live as children of light Ephesians 5:8

I Am

Psalm 1:3
That person is like a tree planted by streams of water, which yields its fruit in season and whose leaf does not wither— whatever they do prospers.

I Am like a tree firmly planted by streams of living water. My leaves do not wither, whatever I put my hand to, will be prosperous.

The Lord was with Joseph so that he prospered, and he lived in the house of his Egyptian master. Genesis 39:2

You will eat the fruit of your labor; blessings and prosperity will be yours. Psalm 128:2

Blessed is the one

Psalm 1:1-2
Blessed is the one who does not walk in step with the wicked or stand in the way that sinners take or sit in the company of mockers, but whose delight is in the law of the Lord, and who meditates on his law day and night.

I will not walk with the wicked. I will turn from my sinful ways. I will do what delights my Lord.

For the Lord God is a sun and shield; the Lord bestows favor and honor; no good thing does he withhold from those whose walk is blameless. Psalms 84:11

I Am

1 John 5:5
Who is it that overcomes the world? Only the one who believes that Jesus is the Son of God.

I Am an Overcomer!

To the one who is victorious, I will give the right to sit with me on my throne, just as I was victorious and sat down with my Father on his throne. Revelation 3:21

Being Me Is Enough

Psalm 23:3-4
he refreshes my soul. He guides me along the right paths for his name's sake. Even though I walk through the darkest valley, I will fear no evil, for you are with me; your rod and your staff, they comfort me.

All Is Well.

I Am A Masterpiece

Because I have the peace of the Master within me!

And a certain scribe came, and said unto Him, Master, I will follow thee whithersoever thou goest. Matthew 8:19